DON'T GO DEEPER!

Forget Consolidation Loans...

Forget Refinance Loans...

Forget Years Of
High Interest
And/Or Fees
(or *other payments*)
Paid To
Credit Counselors Or
Non-Profit Organizations...

Negotiate With Creditors And Bill Collectors
Yourself
To Reduce Your Debts To
PENNIES
ON THE DOLLAR
And Get Out Of Debt Sooner!

by Elaine Silverman

DON'T GO DEEPER!
How To Negotiate With Creditors And Bill Collectors *Yourself* To Reduce Your Debts To Pennies On The Dollar

Copyright ©2008 by Pencraft Publications, LLC

Published by
The Apothecary's Natural Solutions, Inc.
PO Box 1004
Mount Vernon, OH 43050

All rights reserved. No part of this work may be duplicated in any way without express written consent of the publisher and author, except brief passages for purposes of a review. No part of this publication may be stored in a retrieval system, or transmitted in any form or by any means, electronic, mechanical, recording, or otherwise, without prior written permission of the author and publisher.

Printed in the United States of America.

Disclaimer: The material contained in this book is sold to the purchaser as opinion for information and entertainment purposes only, and is not to be construed as official financial advice or service, or legal advice or service. If you are experiencing debt problems, you may need the paid advice and/or service of a competent accountant or attorney.

ISBN 978-0-6152-0773-5

Dedicated to YOU, the reader…

…who feels trapped by the high cost of the "usury" which is draining your energy and your life. This book is published to help you take responsibility for your situation and take action to change it.

My special thanks go to Ken Yarbrough, my instructor, whom I can no longer find to get in touch with. Ken, if you ever get a hold of this and read it, know that so many people are thankful you made this information public so we have a way to deal with the credit issues that are oppressing the people in this country right now. I give credit to you for the knowledge in this book. Thank you for the samples of the letters and conversations.

TABLE OF CONTENTS

Qualifications ……………..…. **11**

Introduction ……………….…. **14**

SECTION I – Understanding How You Got There, And How To Get Away From There ……17

Chapter 1 ………………….…. **19**
History of Credit And Debit: It's Not All Your Fault
    The Powers That Be … 19
    Claim, Not Blame:
    The Power To Change Your Situation … 22

Chapter 2 ……………………... **25**
The Principle Of Prosperity
    A Different Way Of Looking At It … 25
    Do You Really Get What You Deserve? … 27
    A Different Way Of Calculating It … 28
    Your Energy Is Your True Value Of Cost …29

SECTION II - How To Negotiate With Creditors And Bill Collectors To Reduce Your Debts To Pay Only PENNIES On Every Dollar You Owe … 31

Chapter 3 ……………………… **33**
Knowledge Is The Key To Unlocking The Trap Of Debt
    An Eye-Popping Discussion Of Bankruptcy … 34
    The Necessary Frame Of Mind: You Call The Shots … 39
    The Life And Death Of A Debt: How To Tell Where Your Debt Is In The Cycle, What To Do About It … 41

The Secret Agenda Of Collections Agencies : If You Know This Secret, You Can Wrap Them Around Your Little Finger! ... 44

An Expose Of Non-Profit Credit Counseling Services :
How They Make You Pay, Even If They Don't Ask For A Fee ... 46

Re-negotiation : Only Those Who "Do It Yourself" Can Take Advantage Of This ... 48

Chapter 4 51
The Secret 12 Steps To Successful Debt Negotiation

(Includes Examples Of Any Necessary Telephone Conversations)

The First Contact ... 57

Dangling A Carrot And How To Protect Yourself While Doing It ... 63

What To Do If They Don't Settle: Who To Call And Who To Tell ... 65

If A Judgment Is Obtained Against You: Measures You Can Take ... 66

Miscellaneous Tips: Secrets To "Tweak" The System In Your Favor Timing, Credit Rating, Secrecy, Your Rights, Loose Lips, Toot Your Horn, Don't Cry Wolf, Attorneys, *How To Verify Your Debt, and TRULY Get Incorrect Information Erased From Your Credit Report*, Two Debts Are Better Than One, Statute Of Limitations, Verbatim Is Bad ... 68

How To Handle Abuses And Who To Report Them To ... 75

    Who To Tell ... 75

    List Of Abuses Which Are Not Allowed According To The Law ... 76

    How To Handle The Violations ... 79

    The FTC Address And Phone Numbers To Report Violations To ... 80

Chapter 5 ……………………….. 83
Letters And Other Samples
    (Includes Samples Of Any Necessary Letters To Be Written)
    Item A - Net Worth Worksheet … 84
    Item B - Personal Budget Worksheet … 90
    Item C - Settlement Letter #1, Out Of Court Settlement … 93
    Item D - Settlement Letter #2, Out Of Court Settlement … 95
    Item E - Settlement Letter #3, Out Of Court Settlement … 97
    Item F - Harassment Formal Complaint Letter … 98
    Item G - Letter Of Dispute Of A Debt … 100

Chapter 6 ………………………….. 101
RESOURCES
    The Law Pertaining To Debt Collection … 101
    Obtaining A TRULY Free Credit Report … 102

SECTION III – Keeping Your Personal Energy Free … 105

    Conclusion ……………..……. 106

    Suggested Reading ………….. 107

Qualifications And Certifications For This Book

The author, Elaine Silverman, writes from home focusing on practical details for living an enlightened life. Ms. Silverman has been a nationally published contributing editor and writer in industry trade magazines, and currently writes her own newsletter focusing on toxin-free organic foods and related issues.

Experience with personal debt and seemingly insurmountable credit problems inspired Ms. Silverman to investigate and uncover many little known facts surrounding the debt and credit industry today, which the average consumer generally does not have access to.

Becoming immersed in the project of reducing her own debt, she studied to become a Debt Reduction And Credit Consultant, obtaining certification from the *Debt Reduction And Credit Consultant Institute* of Coral Gables, FL. (Debt Reduction And Credit Consultant Institute, Instructor - Mr. Ken Yarbrough.)

She is qualified to *consult* in the areas of credit repair, debt reduction and collection, bankruptcy, and income tax collection activity. This does NOT imply Ms. Silverman is a lawyer or accountant or other licensed financial individual qualified to give legal advice or official advice in any financial area,

however, she has been instructed in the basic laws concerning the Fair Credit Reporting Act, the Consumer Credit Protection Act, The Tax Reform Act, Title III, the Fair Credit Billing Act, the Equal Credit Opportunity Act, The Fair Debt Collection Practices Act, and the IRS Tax Collection Guidelines.

This instruction provides Ms. Silverman with insight and information which can help the average consumer gain knowledge needed to successfully negotiate with creditors, collections agencies, and credit reporting agencies. This information is also useful for implementing credit correction and repair, and for obtaining debt reduction without having to use a commercial consumer's credit agency. Also, in some cases, this information can help the consumer to reduce income tax debt.

In an effort to make known to the public the little known facts about credit, debt, and the financial industry in general, the effects it has on personal lives, and strategies for successfully dealing with the consequences of debt and credit, Ms. Silverman has written this book with the intention that anyone who sincerely wants to know how to "work the system", at least this one aspect of it, should have the information to do it.

INTRODUCTION

Some people in the credit/debt/financial industry do not like the fact I am going to tell you the truth here in this book about the laws which govern your debts. Not necessarily because I will reveal some deep dark secrets, (which I will, because *to you they are*!) but because what I am about to reveal to you goes against what mainstream financial consultants always tell you. Most of them simply parrot one another, and repeat information spewed from one spotlighted financial town-crier to the next. Often, they haven't really studied the laws governing credit or debt, and they don't really know the answers to some of the real-life questions you face when wracked with debt. Often, they haven't checked the true sources of the regulations which govern the information they are conveying.

In this book is some startling information. You will learn not only the industry trade secrets about how to easily and painlessly negotiate to reduce your debts to a fraction of their original amounts, (with your creditors gladly taking what they can get!), you'll learn *why* you can do this. You will understand the laws which govern and protect you as you work to eliminate your debts. You will learn exactly what to do, when, what to say, who to say it to, and how to maneuver the collections agents into sweating it out, hoping you'll be able to come up with *anything* to pay them! You'll learn the psychological head games they purposely play with you, and how to cut them short at the first sign of it.

Some of the other astonishing information you will learn is how the "non-profit" credit counselors are ripping you off. Their ads scream they are non-profit. Their ads scream you do not need to get a loan to reduce your debts, and you may not have to. They even tell you the service is "free". After all, you don't pay them any fee to do this. But don't think for one minute they are *really* working for you... *or anybody*... for FREE. I'll tell you how you are *really* paying them, and the roundabout way they've got their hands in *your pockets*. If you want to use them to do the same thing for you that you will learn how to do in this book, that's fine. But be aware of what you really are paying for that service. I know, because I studied the same information they did and became certified to do the same thing they do. I'll tell you here in this book how to do it yourself, and save yourself the "free" fee. I don't know about you, but if I deal with someone, I'd at least like to be told the truth about how they are managing to financially hold me over a barrel. Keep in mind not all debt reduction services or consolidation services are a swindle. But now you will have the knowledge to understand what is going on, and you'll be able to spot the questionable services.

You will also come to see that there *really is* a way to clean up your credit report and remove valid and true but negative information for good. YES, it can be done, and the folks who tell you it is a scam are incorrect, but they tell you that because they've heard so many "trusted" advisors say it before. Except, watch out here... the folks who want to charge you money to do it for you ARE scamming you, and you will find out why! You will understand the truth about the mechanics of how removing true but negative information can be done as you read the information in this book, because you will get to the source of the issue. You will know the law, and you will see and understand how the law allows for timing, and how other factors work for you to remove that negative information! It isn't always possible, but *it can be done*.

In this book, and in all the publications, free newsletters, and other books which The Apothecary's Natural Resources publishes, I attempt to dig for the truth, ferret it out, and pass it on to you. It is your right to know the truth. I attempt to give you a new perspective on the issues that are important to you, and which are part of the intangible environment that surrounds you and which affect your daily life. It is my hope in reading this book you will come to see a little more of the reality which surrounds you that you have previously been unaware of... the reality of debt and credit, and how to use and eliminate them in your life to free yourself from the bondage of being owned by your possessions, instead of you owning them. It is my goal to enlighten you to a little more of the reality of what goes on around you and affects you without your consent, how you are taken advantage of, and it is my goal to give you the tools you need to realize you no longer have to struggle in ignorance of what you are entitled to.

Section I

Understanding How You Got There, And How To Get AWAY From There

Chapter 1

A Short And Recent History Of Credit And Debt

The Powers That Be

It's not *all* YOUR fault! Although we need to never forget that it is we who originally chose to incur the debt we have, we need to understand there has been a certain amount of targeted interference in our decision to use credit, aimed directly at us. The most obvious is the daily messages bombarding us from the media in the form of commercials on TV and radio, the internet, and print ads in our newspapers and magazines. It is no secret they blatantly tell you to "buy now, pay later".

But some of the scariest harbingers of clandestine motives are also the cruelest, ripping the cash from your pockets before you know what hit you, before it even *gets* to your pockets. This is the income tax, (not my opinion, actually documented in the constitution), and the sly imposition on the American people of a privately owned banking corporation disguising itself as a governmental authority, with the complete blessing of those in power in the government.

Without continuing on this subject, suffice it to say you have been charged interest in the form of taxes so that you can pay for the debt your government owes to private bankers known as the FED, or Federal Reserve System. AND it was planned that way by the German and other European bankers who instituted this private corporation into our economic system. [This information, previously "underground" and considered controversial, has recently come out in the open and been announced on some of the CNN late night talk shows. In particular, Glenn Beck dedicated an entire evening in March of '08 to exposing the fact the Federal Reserve is an elite group of bankers who are not part of the government, and who own the IRS.]

If your government (which is a corporation of and by itself) incurred debts and you paid them *directly* for it through taxes, the Constitution allows for taxing your INTEREST earned on savings and investments, NOT your *income*, to pay for this debt. (The FED decided they would make out better if they LEND the American government the money to pay for their debts, than ALSO charged interest ON that debt by taxing the American people's gross income.) The INTEREST on that debt ALWAYS accumulates, and therefore the debt is NEVER PAID... and therefore, you will always pay income tax.

In addition, because the FED is the largest and strongest privately owned corporation that exists, their control filters down to all the banks in our economic system. Some are owned by FED shareholders and others are not. Either way, they are all tied in together. The abundance of credit available to you and me and the interest we pay to our credit cards and on other bank loans today are devices to earn profits in the pockets of the FED... as if they don't have enough of our taxed income already.

You see, to put it succinctly, you have been hogwashed into believing you need credit to get what you want, and it has been done to you on purpose. The people who control the media are themselves controlled by the people who control the bank, the FEDERAL RESERVE SYSTEM. By "controlled I mean the media companies are owned by the same elite few that control the banking system.

These kind folks bombard us with "get it now" ads, then take it from us twice and three times in the form of sales taxes and credit card interest we pay, as well as income taxes. And, *we **let** them*. How? If you borrowed money in the form of a loan or through a credit card, it was *your choice*, and you have to pay the credit card or loan interest, because you agreed to the contract they gave it to you under. **And unless you and they agree together to change that contract, you are bound by it.**

So when you choose to make that credit purchase, large or small, because you feel you have no choice when the kid needs braces or the car broke down, know that you are not making that choice totally alone. You've been pushed into doing it, through a carefully thought out plan and design to make it easy for you to do. (The scope of this plan and design is almost unfathomable, almost unbelievable, and not within the reach of this book to unveil.)

Claim, Not Blame
The Power To Change Your Situation

BUT, you are the one with the final say in the matter. You don't have to respond to that button being pushed. At least not in the way of using more credit. There is always an alternative. You are the one who gives your consent to agree to pay for the item/service you are purchasing, and to pay for it at least two times, maybe three or more times over, in the end. You are the one who willingly succumbs to the ads to have what you think is valuable *now*. Your energy is what you really are "spending" when you use money to have something. <u>You are the one</u> who - when you incur a debt by borrowing money, for *anything* - <u>promises away your future energy</u> *to have what you want now.* Do you agree with that? If you do, this is good news that you do, because it is true.

Before you can pick yourself up out of any debt dilemma you're in, you need to be able to take responsibility for having gotten yourself there in the first place. Why? If you can admit you have done it to yourself, and claim the responsibility for the result, then you automatically give yourself the power to do something "different" to un-do the mess you are in. If, on the other hand you *blame* someone else or something else for your situation, (even if they've had a hand in it!) you are agreeing to leave your destiny in *their* capable hands, until they (or it) decide to change your life for you.

Take the road of responsibility, which gives you the power to take action and change what you don't like. If you decide not to and blame others or something else instead for your circumstances, then don't complain about your situation, as you are creating it yourself with your own inaction.

Chapter 2

The Principle Of Prosperity

A Different Way Of Looking At It

Without making slight of your situation, as that is not intended, consider transforming your emotional pattern of thoughts in all areas of your life, especially in the areas of finance. A simple way to do this is to transform the words you use when thinking and talking about your situation. What you focus on is what you attract to you, and by continually thinking about your problem of debt and how little you have, you are focusing on exactly that and bringing more of that into your life.

If, on the other hand, you focus on the solution to debt, and think about implementing the solution and how good it will feel not to have the debt, that is what you will attract to your life. Personally, I always think about how good it feels to live without debt and to have all debts paid, with no future energy promised out. If I were to think about *how good it will feel when* I am *finally out of debt*, I would still be attracting the debt to stay in my life because I am *focusing on the fact I am not really out of debt yet.* Instead, in your thoughts as you imagine your future, imagine it as if you were already living it, not always looking for it at a distant time.

Begin by completely eliminating any conversation which places you as the victim. As we just learned, if you continue to believe you are a victim, you will never have the power to change what you don't like about your current situation. After that, continue by changing the words you use when you think or talk about your situation. If you use words that are emotionally intensive, your perception of your situation will reflect that. If you use words which are more tolerant of your situation, and even more positive, your attitude will reflect that change, and after your attitude changes, so then will the situation be able to follow suit. But only then!

For instance, if you think of or talk about your situation as "devastating", the it is. Isn't it? The emotion tied to that word is very intense. If you look at your situation as merely "disappointing", (and it is disappointing!), you have changed the emotional intensity. Your mind begins to clear, your ideas begin to flow, and your attitude begins to create a solution. If you look at the same exact situation as simply "annoying", you have the freedom to move away from the idea "it's being done to me!" to "what can I do to change this".

Yes, your situation can be grave. Yes, it can be emotionally intense. That is probably why you bought this book and are seeking to learn how to reduce your debts to a manageable amount. If you add to the knowledge you'll learn in the second part of this book the change in the frame of mind you need as explained above, you'll have the ability, energy, and endurance you will need to accomplish your task.

Do You Really Get What You Deserve?

Yes, we all deserve what we get. The secret is, we decide what we deserve, and that's exactly what we get. The following quote on the flow of abundance in your life is from Dr. Wayne Dyer, in his book **You'll See It When You Believe It**.

> "Whatever you enjoy receiving in your life, remind yourself, "I deserve this". It is okay to feel deserving. And you will if you believe the self that is receiving something is worthy and important. Abundance is related to how you feel about yourself. If you feel you are important enough to ask and [and to] receive, receiving will be your reward. If, on the other hand, you feel unworthy, it will be almost impossible for abundance to flow into your life. Think of how a tree unfolds to all of it's magnificent potential, always reaching for the sunshine and growing and flourishing. Would you ever suggest to a tree, "You should be ashamed of yourself for having that disgusting moss on your bark, and for letting your limbs grow crooked"? Of course not. A tree *allows* the life force to work through it. You have the power within your thoughts to be as natural as that tree. I often remind myself of this by recalling something Lao-

Tze once said, thousands of years ago: "The snow goose need not bathe to make itself white. Neither need you to do anything but be yourself."

A Different Way Of Calculating It

No matter how hard you try, a budget won't work. There is a reason! A budget has the emotional and psychological impact of *restriction*. You are always focusing on what you *do not have* in order to contain what you do have. With this kind of mentality, you will never have enough! And you will get tired of knowing that, and you will resent it and spend you way into mounds of more debt. It is done by thousands of people, not just you.

Before you can get yourself OUT of debt, you need to be certain you will not be accruing more debt or simply just defeating your purpose by spending on credit and getting yourself back INTO debt. When you can finally begin to understand exactly what money is, not just in it's physical value, then and only then will you have the burning desire to do whatever it takes to get your money working for *you*, instead of you working for *it*.

If you have found you can't seem to control your spending, and budgets don't work, or budgets are of no use to you because you have no money leftover after the bills are paid, I recommend you purchase a book entitled **Your Money Or Your Life** which will transform your relationship with your money, guaranteed.

Your Energy Is Your True Value Of Cost

When you can look at money as an exchange for your life energy, then you can begin to understand you trade your life energy for the things you buy. You spend your life's energy (by working) in exchange for money, and then you use that money to buy the things you want. Take that money out of the picture, and you can begin to see you need to value the things you buy with your money in a very different way to give you a clearer picture of how you relate to the things you buy.

Add to that the fact you spend MORE energy to accumulate the amount of money it takes to buy something, other than just the hour it took you to earn the agreed upon wage you received, and you will begin to view your wants and desires in a different light. For example, you spend time (which equals energy, when you are spending it) to get ready for work, to shop for the clothes you need to dress for work in, to do so many things, just to get that wage for that one hour. In terms of the time it takes you to shop and dress for that one hour, how much money did you spend (in terms of your energy) to get one hour's wage in return? Now, when you spend money on a thing (or service), how much did you *really* pay for it?

The book **Your Money Or Your Life: Transforming Your Relationship With Money And Achieving Financial Independence** teaches you how to equate those things ... how to calculate the true value of your time and energy, and how to calculate the true cost of whatever you buy with the money you've earned.

You learn the three questions which will transform your life, and how to answer and interpret them: 1) Did I receive fulfillment, satisfaction, and value in proportion for the life energy spent? 2) Is this expenditure of my life energy in alignment with my values and life purpose? and 3) How might this expenditure change if I didn't have to work for a living?

You'll be taught how to make your life energy visible, and how to achieve your dream lifestyle on a shoestring... how to value your life energy and gladly, willfully, deliberately, and easily minimize your spending. You'll also learn how to value your life energy to maximize your income. You'll get the nine magical steps to create a completely new and different road map for your life and your finances, which you can use as you begin to eliminate the debt from your life with the information you will discover in this book which you are reading now. I highly recommend you purchase **Your Money Or Your Life** as soon as possible and use it in conjunction with this debt reduction information. The book is entitled **Your Money Or Your Life: Transforming Your Relationship With Money And Achieving Financial Independence**, written by Joe Dominguez and Vicki Robin, and is published by Penguin Books.

Section II

How To Reduce Your Debts To Pay Only PENNIES On Every Dollar You Owe

Chapter 3

Knowledge Is The Key To Unlocking The Trap Of Debt

Sometimes a collection agency has no choice but to accept payment of only pennies on the dollar for certain accounts. Was this luck for the people involved? Was this an unusual circumstance? No, it's just one of the best kept secrets in the industry. You can pull the strings in your own favor to create the same situation and circumstances and results for yourself, with the right knowledge and a mixture of a few other ingredients such as timing, consistency, and the right frame of mind.

Knowledge is power! When you know what the law is, when you know what your bill collectors can and can't do, you are in a position to "even up the odds" into your favor. You can stop and indeed *prevent abuses against* you and your account, and you can use the laws in your favor, instead of letting the collection agencies and creditors use your ignorance of the laws in their favor. In the game of debt and credit collections and reduction, whoever knows the most about the other side usually wins. This book will reveal to you all you need to know about your opponents - the creditors and collectors - to help you gain the edge you need to succeed in reducing and eliminating your debts.

In this book you will even up your odds and learn about the life of a debt from creation to completion. You will learn about the importance of consistency, timing, correct frame of mind, and professionalism in the game of debt reduction. And you will learn the 12 steps involved in negotiating a deal and how to create a game plan to use in your personal journey on your way to **a life free from debt and the use of credit... a life where you own what you have, not where what you have owns you.**

An Eye-Popping Discussion Of Bankruptcy

While it is not within the scope of this particular book to discuss the mechanics of bankruptcy, (and the laws are slightly different depending on what state you are in), something must be said about the issue of choosing bankruptcy vs. choosing to work on reducing your debts to a manageable amount.

Before any path is chosen, a look at whether you feel it is a moral issue to "not pay your bills" is in order. Some folks have a problem with what they term is a moral issue - to not pay a bill as agreed. I understand that, and I also would have a problem with that.

A brief explanation of credit and debt history and the true identity of the corporation called the "Federal Reserve" is included in the beginning of this book. When this book was first printed in the early 90's, it was not easy to research that fact except in a library, and only if you knew what book to look in. Now, in 2008, and with the advent of the Internet, the fact that the Federal Reserve is a privately owned corporation working in tandem with the U.S. government is easy to validate. That validation should be all that is needed to convince you that re-negotiating your contract with that company of how you pay the bill is quite acceptable. After all, it is a corporation, not representatives of the people of the United States. What you feel about it is your choice, but if you realize you will be re-negotiating a contract with a company, and they choose to accept the new terms of your negotiation, you are simply entering into a new agreed upon contract, accepted by both parties, willingly. Is that "wrong"?

Basically, and this is from experience as well as from information culled from informed sources, bankruptcy is not the quick and easy solution some people seem to think it is.

Some may feel bankruptcy is no big deal. Ads are plastered all over the media screaming at you to get the credit you deserve (and if you read section 1, you know what that really means!). You get streams of applications in the mail begging you to request this or that credit card. You can still buy a home. You can still buy a car. You can still DO all of those things, at the cost of putting yourself back into the trap of paying five to ten times more for the privilege of having those things which are so normal in society today. Yes you CAN still get and have those possessions and services.

But after you've gotten out of the trap of paying perpetual interest on your credit by filing bankruptcy, you are no better off. If you again patronize the use of credit, you still pay the high cost of your bad decisions to get into debt in the first place, because *now you are a risk* to the credit card companies. (Or they want you to think that, anyway.) You are a "risk" with NO LEGAL WAY OUT NOW, since you cannot claim bankruptcy again for another 7 years. Duh! Of COURSE they are going to give you credit again, (with an interest rate which matches the national debt because remember, you are a "risk"), because they know you HAVE NO CHOICE now but to PAY, no matter how much debt you rack up this time. **And this time it's easier to rack it up faster, because your "risk" interest rates are sky high.**

Get real. In this life, you PAY for your mistakes, no matter how smooth it looks on the surface. What is that famous cliché? "Burn me once, shame on you... burn me twice shame on ME!". (Always remember you are NOT the victim, and you made your choice to engage in using your future life's energy to have possessions now, thereby racking up debt). DON'T allow yourself to be burned again!

The final injustice is when you are led to believe you NEED to re-establish your credit. **WHO really NEEDS to put themselves in a position of allowing the life to be squeezed of out them a second time after they've had it squeezed out once already?** Who really NEEDS to fall into the habit again of living above their means, and working for their money, instead of making changes which will get their money working for them? Do you really NEED credit? No, not at all. But you, the small and ignorant working class (in their opinion, not mine) are made to believe that you NEED to owe the big banks money or something is not right in your life. Why? Ask yourself, do the big bankers live up to their noses with credit debt just to have what they have? Of course not! They get all they need from YOU and your interest payments, because you believed them when they told you that YOU NEED to owe them money, and have "credit".

Bankruptcy keeps you from renting the apartment

you want, when your prospective landlord checks your credit record. Bankruptcy keeps you from getting the home you want when you are a credit risk. Bankruptcy keeps you from getting the job you need, when your prospective employer checks your credit records. Bankruptcy keeps you from getting the insurance you need, even car insurance, when the company checks your credit history. Bankruptcy hurts you in many ways you don't realize, even years after you have forgotten about it.

Your bankruptcy records are legally available to anyone within the industry or position of those cited above, as well as phone companies, utility companies, and others, who, although obligated by law to allow you those services, also make you pay for the privilege and "risk" of taking you on by charging you incredibly large deposit sums, sometimes into the multiple hundreds of dollars, before extending you the service.

For more information about bankruptcy, you can usually meet with a local attorney for a free consultation. When you do, remember that bankruptcy is NOT a quick or easy solution to all your financial troubles, so don't let a fast talking lawyer try to convince you it is. If your debt is less than the equivalent of one year's net income plus the cash equivalent of the possessions which would be included in the bankruptcy, it is probably easier for you to reduce your debts to a manageable amount (and the information in this book will tell you how to do it) than to file for bankruptcy. (Yes, you will have to give some possessions back when filing bankruptcy, in some cases.)

Also be aware that although the law seems to fluctuate on this point, it is possible that the IRS will want you to pay taxes on the amount of your forgiven debt when you claim bankruptcy. An attorney can counsel you as to whether that law is current in your state or not.

There is no such thing as debtors prison. But there is a felony charge for not paying your TAXES! And with the felony charge comes, you guessed it, prison.

While it is not within the scope of this particular book to either debate or explain the entire method or technique that can be used to claim "sovereignty", at which point the laws of the corporation of the United States will not apply to you, be aware that it is possible to be sovereign and live outside the spectrum of it's laws (in regards to payment of debt and bankruptcy). For that to be possible, you must not enter into any contracts of commerce which would make you then subject to those laws. In other words, *have no debt*.

Also be aware, if you are in debt from a loan or credit card, then you entered into a contract in which you agree to the debt for which you are responsible as a "subject" (or technically, as a "possession" of) of the United States. Using the laws which govern its "subjects" will probably be the easiest way to change the contract you have to pay the debt, either by bankruptcy, or by negotiation to change the contract. This book is about how to change the contract by negotiation between you, a subject of the corporation of the U. S., and whatever corporation you entered into the contract with when you accepted your loan (or credit card) and signed the papers.

In conclusion, you can almost always settle your account for a fraction of the original amount, and barring any unusual circumstances which would require a bankruptcy, it is in your best interest to do so. Deal directly with your creditors, or at least their collections agencies, and you can save yourself a headache in the long run. If you do eventually file for bankruptcy, it is in your best interest to first attempt to reduce the payments and pay the debts.

The Necessary Frame Of Mind
You Call the Shots

Before you begin, it is essential you understand something about the type of individual the debt collector is, and the type of individual you must become if you are not already (or at least make the collections agent think you are), to accomplish your desired outcome.

The debt collector is a wage earner and working for a living. The debt collector is doing a job, and that job necessitates the collector to be brief, blunt, and unemotional, at least when it comes to hearing your "side" of the "story". The collector has heard every excuse imaginable, and in reality, your excuses don't matter. (The collector will use emotion against you, but not be affected by it when you try to appeal to him or her.)

You must remember here, YOU are NOT the victim. YOU chose to accept the credit extended to you by the creditor, and agreed to prompt payment and compliance with their terms and conditions. At least for today in these United States, no one held a gun to your head and forced you to accept credit. ("There is ALWAYS an alternative" - Captain Picard) When you fail to pay promptly, and do not comply with the terms and conditions of the agreement you made, you find yourself up against the creditor's house policy of debt collection, later combined with the indifferent and imperturbable attitude of the collector assigned to your "case".

That collector has hundreds of other cases just like yours, and is required to follow a procedure to attempt to collect the debt you owe. Some things you say will work, and some won't, unless you know the right things to say, and when. Take the responsibility for your actions (of using credit, and not being able to pay) and deal with it in a matter-of-fact way. Use professionalism in your responses to collectors. We will deal with the details of real or implied threats later, but for now know that you MUST respond with knowledge and courteousness. It is imperative if you want to reduce the debt, no matter how much of a turkey the collector is. They STILL hold all the cards in your deal, for now.

HERE, you'll learn which things work and which won't. Here you'll learn the procedures and processes necessary to accomplish your end. Here, you'll need a cool head, an undaunted attitude, and you'll also need to leave the sob stories elsewhere. And you especially have to resolve to not take anything "personally", because it isn't. If you get a faint heart at the sound of a raised voice, and an emotional "poor me" attitude, get over it if you want to get out of debt.

You don't need to take any verbal abuse, but you'll need to know how to stop it before it starts, and be able to. You can't do that if you're in an emotional pile on the floor, or in a rage. It is best to view your dealings with collectors in the matter of reducing your debt as a business deal, which it IS to them. It will be easier for you to keep your cool, keep your courage, and get what you want.

Collections agencies are wary of debtors who know their rights and show no fear. They tend to back off and stay away from certain "gray areas" when dealing with a person who obviously knows what he or she is talking about. You knowledge is your edge, and the collector knows this. It will make the process of debt reduction easier for the both of you.

The correct frame of mind is perhaps your most

vital tool in debt reduction. Your image must radiate through your voice, and the collector on the other end must get the impression that you are firm, determined, not afraid, and yet at the same time humble, honest, and willing to work like a team to do the right thing. (Yes, I said HUMBLE. Remember you are NOT the victim here, you did not pay as you gave your word you would.) Above all, remember the person collecting wants to control your emotions through fear. They play a psychological game, they know it, and they do it well. Don't let them affect you.

The Life And Death Of A Debt
How To Tell Where Your Debt Is In The Cycle
What To Do About It

A creditor, as mentioned above, has certain in-house policies for dealing with a past-due debt. These policies are designed to collect the debt with the least amount of expense, and to preserve the good will of the creditor. The idea is to collect the most with the least amount of effort. Before you begin to understand how to deal with your creditor and collections agencies, you must understand the unseen process your debt has gone through, in an attempt to accomplish this.

When your account is one month delinquent, it means no payment was received within the past 30 days. You may receive a separate letter from the creditor reminding you of this, or you may receive a notice on your next month's statement. Typically, most people who receive these reminders either lost the bill, forgot, or temporarily had no money. When the reminder arrives, or the next statement is received, the bill is paid. The creditors know this, and they don't panic. Credit card companies actually LOVE when you pay late. They lie in wait and use this as an excuse to slap you with both a late payment fee AND raise your interest rate.

When an account has not received any payment for the past 60 days, (two 30 day billing cycles), the account is considered two months delinquent. The creditor is still very interested in maintaining the debtor as a customer, because the creditor still wants the customer to patronize him, after he pays. The creditor is careful here not to scare, intimidate, or embarrass the customer. At this point, the customary procedure is to begin a sequence of formal letters, usually about 15 days apart. If no payment or response is received, a phone call will be made to ask if something "is wrong".

At the three months delinquent point, when payment has not been received for the past three 30-day billing cycles, it is understood by the creditor that he has a serious collection problem. It is a known fact that the longer a debt is overdue, the harder it is to collect. In this stage, the pace is stepped up with more phone calls and formal letters. The creditor is not so interested in preserving the customer as a patron any more, and will use all in-house means available to collect the debt.

In-house credit managers find it highly undesirable to turn a debt over to a collection agency, for three reasons. One, they will lose a percentage of the amounts owed. Two, they may feel as if they were incompetent in their job, and they are afraid their superiors may feel this way. And three, public relations considerations. This knowledge will work in your favor, if your debt has not gone to an agency for collections, yet.

If the credit of the debtor has not been rescinded yet, it will be now. The debtor is advised, somewhere in the fourth month of being past due, that the debt is being handed over to a collections agency or an attorney for collection. The creditor no longer wants the debtor as a customer, and declares "open season" and makes plans to collect what is owed to him. If the amount is small, it is usually handed over to a collections agency. If the amount is large, or if the collections agency was unsuccessful and the amount owed is large enough, it is handed over to an attorney for litigation.

Collections agencies are not interested in preserving goodwill; they want to collect. A collections agency will earn between 15% to 60% of the amount collected. The more they collect, the more they make, of course, and the happier their client, the creditor, is. Collections agencies specialize in collecting, and they streamline their collections efforts to accomplish this with the least amount of cost and effort. But perhaps the biggest advantage the agency has over you is psychological. You automatically understand and accept that NOW you are dealing with some really tough guys who don't play games! Right? Suddenly, your "credit history" and "credit report" are threatened, and your knees begin to shake!

Most people will pay the bill at the first sight of the formal letter which initiates the collections agency's introductory contact with the customer. If the debtor does not pay within the next 15 days, up to two more final demand/final notice letters will be received. Sometime after this 15-day time period the calls start coming on the telephone as well. If the debt is less than $100, usually no calls are made, as it is not cost-effective. If the debt is large, the calls will come even before the first letter in the 15-day period is received.

Collections agencies love to make telephone calls for two reasons: one, they can say and insinuate things on the telephone which they would not put in writing because they know it's illegal to "threaten" you, and two, because the telephone is a more personal instrument than a letter. You hear the sound of a real person's voice and are emotionally effected by it. Later you will learn how easy it is to stop annoying phone calls simply by asking, and with just one sentence.

(Before you get any ideas here, it is illegal to record a phone conversation without the prior consent of the person on the other line. AND, you must have the consent within the recording, at the beginning of the conversation. So, if you want to turn on the tape recorder, go ahead. Legally, simply ask permission to keep it on. If they say no, turn it off. But keep that record of that part of the conversation.)

If you do not pay the debt by this time, you can expect a barrage of telephone calls and letters combined, and each one will escalate the seriousness and repercussions of non-payment. Later we'll go into the details of the Fair Debt Collection Practices Act, and how to file a violation of your rights with both the Federal Trade Commission and the attorney general of your state, but for now you should know that this Act protects your rights and prohibits collections agencies from various outrageous collections practices of the past.

The Secret Agenda Of Collections Agencies
If You Know This Secret, You Can Wrap Them Around Your Little Finger!

When dealing with collections agencies, it is to your advantage to see things from their point of view, and understand what a collector is thinking, and why.

First, collectors are in the business of making money for themselves, and are not in the business of collecting the most money for their client (your creditor) at any expense. Sometimes these two objectives end up being one and the same, but if not, the priority is still to maximize profitability by – again – using the least amount of time and money to collect the most. So, what does that mean for you? Think about this: if a collector can collect 70% of a debt with an average time investment of one hour, will it be worth it to the collector to try to get the remaining 30% if spending additional hours will be needed to do it? NO!

And, if you add to that equation the other factors which make a debt potentially "uncollectable", such as the debtor has no assets, is judgment proof, has no income, disappears, or declares bankruptcy, **the collections agency is actually very happy to get what they can, and as quickly as they can.**

Keep this in mind. For these two reasons, **most collections agencies will settle for 50 cents on the dollar! Fifty percent settlements are the accepted rule in the business**. It is quick with little or no effort. The debtor got a great deal. The collector converts the account into cash and closes the books. Although payments can be arranged, a quick settlement for CASH gets the best value in the deal, and the STARTING POINT is 50 cents on the dollar when you can offer a lump sum of CASH as a settlement!

Of course, if you are in financial trouble already, you more than likely don't have that cash. If you don't, payments are an option, but one which collections agencies don't really want to deal with. Even here, you'll pay through the nose by getting less of a deal, just because you have to make payments. After all, if you defaulted this far, the collections agency knows you will typically make two to three payments, and no more. On the other hand, if you choose to or have to make payments, you can always go back and renegotiate, and that would be to your advantage.

Typically in the industry, it is noted by the Debt Reduction And Credit Consultant Institute, that if your account is still with the creditor and has not gone to a collections agency yet, (meaning your account is less than 90 days overdue), your creditor's in-house collections will prefer payments, and with 100 cents-on-the-dollar. If the collector handling your case is inexperienced, this will be especially true. Their experience has also shown that in-house credit managers who are women, either with or without experience, also tend to prefer payments totaling 100 cents-on-the-dollar.

An Expose Of Non-Profit Credit Counseling Services
How They Make You Pay,
Even If They Don't Ask For A Fee!

Let's pause here for a moment to examine the non-profit credit counseling services which are popping up everywhere, proclaiming to lower your debt with no loan involved and no fees. Just so you know, *you are learning the very same information here which they use to reduce your debts.* But what they are NOT telling you is that although you may not need to get a loan (which was an old technique these services used to use, but most no longer do) to consolidate and pay off your debts, you STILL PAY THEM to do this! THINK! Would YOU work without getting paid? Just because a service says it is non-profit, does not mean they do not get paid! HOW do they get paid? You just found out!

What these services have done is set themselves up as the mediators between you and the collections agency or the creditor, and don't think for one minute they don't get paid! They sometimes have pre-arranged agreements with various creditors and collections agencies to accept a certain percentage of your debt as payment for negotiating this deal, and YOU are paying for it. Whether there is a pre-made arrangement or not, they offer the accepted 50 percent, and when it is accepted, charge you 60 percent, or whatever amount more they choose. The point is, they reduce your debt, then add their cut, and pass the cost on to you. You DO get a deal, but you may get a better one by doing it yourself, if you have the guts to try.

What did we learn about the secret agenda of collections agencies? They are in business to make money for themselves, at the least expense in time and money in return for the most payment from you on the debt. These mediators do the same thing, only they are just ONE MORE MIDDLEMAN taking another cut, another percentage from the monthly payment YOU will make, and that naturally translates into YOU paying more out of your pocket than you have to, and paying it longer.

RE-Negotiation
Only Those Who "Do It Yourself" Can
Take Advantage Of This

Instead of letting someone else negotiate for you, do it yourself with the instructions that follow, and you will be able to negotiate for the LOWEST amount on the dollar, sometimes as low as 25 cents on the dollar, or even less. You won't be paying more than you need to just to pay someone to do it for you, *for the life of your debt!* That's right, as long as you make payments, part of it is the percentage which goes to the mediator. Keep it for yourself and pay your debts off SOONER! Here's how...

If you can KEEP it AND lower your debt, then when you get that first debt paid off, RENEGOTIATE THE OTHERS! Things change, and when you negotiate to reduce your debts, more cash is immediately available to you. Stash some... no matter how small. I mean really small! $5 a week will do, if that's all you can. When you get that FIRST debt paid off, add that payment you usually made to your stash. You now have more cash to work with, and are in a position to ask for a lower cents-on-the-dollar amount on one or more of your OTHER debts because now you *negotiate to pay a cash lump sum, and pay less cents-on-the-dollar.*

First, pick your smallest debt and re-negotiate that one. Work your way up to your largest debt from your smallest, re-negotiating each time. Only when you renegotiate, you will be negotiating to pay it off in a lump sum. You will find yourself out of debt much sooner, and you'll be keeping the money you earned for YOUR pockets instead of stuffing it in someone else's. This is how they will do it for you, only you'll be paying them for each month of debt you make payments for! They will only negotiate for you one time, but you can negotiate for a lower cents-on-the-dollar rate to start with, and then re-negotiate again when you have even a small lump sum of cash to pay off some of the others.

The information you are learning here in regards to negotiating and dealing with creditors and collections agencies is the same information these mediators know. The difference between this book and them is the regulation which requires anyone who gets paid for a service of dispensing financial services must be bonded.

This book is not performing a service, and it is not advice. It is simply my opinion of the information. I personally am not performing the service for you, and that's why I do not have to be bonded to tell you this. MY business is selling you a book of opinion/information which you have purchased, for your entertainment, NOT servicing you by arranging for your debt to be reduced. But I have gone through the same training as the credit counseling services, and here in this book you have the same knowledge which you can use to finally and truly be in total control of your own future and your own finances, yourself, without paying continually for someone else to do it.

Chapter 4

The Secret 12 Steps To Successful Debt Negotiation Your Game Plan

1) Begin by taking stock of how much you owe, and to whom. List all your bills... creditors... on a piece of paper. Pull all your monthly statements, collection letters, and all other related information. Sort and stack them into piles for each creditor.

2) Go through each pile for each creditor, and put everything in chronological order, the oldest last, the newest items on the top of the pile. Buy some cardboard file boxes if necessary, with file folders or pockets, and begin to get these things in order. Put each pile in the file folders that way, and file them in the box to keep them close at hand when needed, and organized so you can grab something quick if necessary.

3) Summarize all your debts. Add them all up on a sheet of paper. Determine if it is more or less than your annual income. If it is more, you may want to seriously consider the subject of bankruptcy. This summary is referred to as your "scorecard".

If your accumulated debts are less than the net value of your yearly income, in addition to the sum of the value of the possessions you are willing to give up, then you will probably benefit more from using this debt negotiation information you are reading now than going through bankruptcy. You can use this information to negotiate to reduce your debts, and then combine it with the computerized software system at www.paxeon.com to pay down the amount of the debts left with simple interest instead of compounded interest. (You can also use that system alone, without negotiating.)

4) Fill out the NET WORTH WORKSHEET (Item A) and the PERSONAL BUDGET WORKSHEET (Item B) which are included in the next section. You must do this as **you must know what you have to work with!** You cannot negotiate a deal to pay something you don't know if you have or not. And, in this process, you sometimes find items or services you pay for which you are willing to do without to help yourself out of the situation you are in.

5) Have a meeting with your spouse or whomever you share these debts with. Look over the worksheets you have just created and analyze what resources you have that you can use to pay off some debt. Add up what assets you have that you are willing to sell or refinance to liquidate some outstanding debt. How much cash could you raise in 30 or 60 or 90 days? If you waited longer than 30 days, could you raise more? Or, would that not be a significant amount even if you waited 90 days? Examine all the possibilities and consider everything.

6) Once you have determined what cash you have

available and what cash you are sure you could accumulate by selling or refinancing within a reasonable amount of time, compare that to your debt. Will you really be prepared to make sacrifices to get rid of your debt? Would you prefer to get a part time job instead, or in addition to selling your boat? You get the idea...

7) According to the information you have already learned about the "life and death of a debt", analyze each current debt, and the person or agency who is collecting your debt. Has your debt already been forwarded to a collections agency? Does the creditor still have an interest in maintaining you as a customer? Are they in the same town or country as you are? Make careful notes of all of this information on the front of each file folder for each creditor. Also keep detailed records in each folder of each contact, meaning any letter you sent or received, or any phone conversation and it's date and time and what was said, as each of these things occurs. Use all this information to analyze your creditor or collector, and to determine where you are in the life cycle of the debt. You'll then know more about what that creditor is thinking about you and your debt, and better equip yourself to negotiate.

8) Create and review your game plan.

Let's talk about some things you can do to formulate your game plan here. Remember a creditor *will only accept pennies on the dollar if he or she believes not one cent more can be collected.* A collector will stop fighting and settle for less IF: a) debtor is judgment proof b) debtor has no money c) debtor makes collector believe he has no money or items of value.
Do what you can to judgment proof yourself so that your assets are protected. If you have a substantial

amount of money in a bank account, it will be found. (Note: if you are seriously considering filing for bankruptcy, your financial dealings as well as your purchases, and the amount of money you've had in the bank, for the past six months, up to three years in some cases, is examined. You will need the advice of a competent bankruptcy lawyer for this.

9) Once you've made your decisions about how to restructure your accounts or finances, if at all, and taken those steps, it is time to call the creditors. Always conduct yourself in a professional manner. Following is a checklist to help you prepare before your call, and to help you during and after the call. Following this checklist will be a sample conversation script.

_____ You must remember at all times that it is critically essential that you make your collections agent understand that unless a reasonable settlement can be made with **ALL** of your creditors, you will have no choice but to file for bankruptcy.

BANKRUPTCY is hated by collections agents because they know the creditor will end up with either NOTHING or at the most two to three cents on the dollar, and the collection agency with less for all their time and trouble spent. Often the agency does not even get paid at all after a bankruptcy. *Bankruptcy is your most powerful weapon.*
(And it is also one reason why credit card companies scramble to offer you high interest rate cards after you've been through a bankruptcy. Often, it's the same companies whom you've just filed against. They want to charge you high interest to recoup their losses on you, and they KNOW you can't shaft them again for another 7 years at least! By that time, at the interest

rates they charge you, they've made more than their losses back from you. DON'T FALL FOR IT!

Use the threat of bankruptcy in your favor, *but only if it is real,* **and if you are seriously considering it.** It is especially powerful if you mention the name of a local attorney you have met with or are considering meeting with, but you don't have to.

_____Prepare a list for yourself of the points you wish to cover when speaking with the collection agent. Have the list with you when you call, and take notes about what was said in regard to each point when you call.

_____Think about some objections you think the creditor may make, and write down responses to those objections. All of your responses should match your game plan.

_____Practice what you are going to say. Go over it first in your mind, and see yourself saying the things you plan to say, and see the collection agent agreeing. You may even wish to role play with your spouse or someone else. (We'll give you an idea of what to say on the first contact with a collections agent in a moment.)

_____Pause before answering any questions... ALWAYS. Before you open your mouth, repeat the question to yourself mentally. The agent will try to throw you off track, so be sure to have your checklist and game plan written down in front of you. If you are asked something you do not want to answer, or are not sure how to answer, (and even the nicest collections agent will do this to you!) tell the agent you need to check with your attorney, accountant, or spouse. In other words, put the answer off on someone else who is not available at the time.

_____After your first call, sit back and analyze your results. It was most likely not a bad experience, as collectors at this point are usually nice. Make any modifications necessary to the game plan, and call the next one.

_____Always make your calls at a time when you can give the collector your undivided attention on the phone with absolutely no interruptions.

_____Always be courteous and polite, and even apologetic, (remember YOU owe THEM money, not the other way around!) BUT don't let yourself be open to harassment. An experienced collections agent will not become abusive if you are working together and they see progress.

_____*Don't let on you know what you know.* Don't sound overly knowledgeable or very polished in collections matters. The only time you need to be aggressive with your knowledge is if the collector begins to harass you. And then, you MUST remain cool headed and polite, even when you are letting the agent know you will not tolerate harassment and will file a complaint against them with the Federal Trade Commission and the state attorney.

_____**NEVER offer any type of settlement on the first contact call to a collections agent. NEVER agree to any type of settlement on the first contact call**. Remember, you must check with your attorney, accountant, or spouse.

_____At the end of your conversation, *before you hang up*, summarize what you agreed upon, also on what you did not agree upon, and make a phone appointment with the date and time you will be calling back. Make the date and time for approximately two to three weeks. (Approximately… when it is convenient for YOU.) Be in control of the first call. Do not let the collector push for an earlier second contact. Do not agree to do it their way, *whatever* they ask. Tell the collector that your attorney or accountant is a busy person and it will take that long before you can get back to them.

The First Contact

Advise the collections agent you are in the process of contacting all your creditors to see what kind of realistic program can be set up for the repayment of your debts. A phone conversation might go something like this:

"Hello, Mr. Jones, my name is _____. I am calling regarding account number _____.

First, I want to apologize for not getting back to you sooner. [*remember, you've gotten collections letters already!*] I had put off this call because I was waiting to see if I got hired for a job I applied for so I could begin to pay my debts. [*Use whatever applies to you here, if it's not a job. Maybe sickness, or divorce, or whatever. But indicate you had hoped something would work out but it did not.*] Unfortunately, I was not hired, and frankly I have very limited resources. [<u>*Always add and stress*</u> that you have limited funds, continually.]

[*It does not hurt here to BRIEFLY explain your particular situation or circumstance, ... loss of job, sickness, failed business... but <u>don't get involved in a sob story</u>. You want the collector to know your claim is valid, but you don't want to say too much about it.*]

My attorney, Mr. _____ has advised me to file for bankruptcy. I told him I would like to leave bankruptcy as a final solution and hopefully avoid it altogether. I am in the process of contacting all my creditors to see what can be done. I will call you in a week from Tuesday [*or whenever you decide*] to advise you of my progress.

Meanwhile, please contact [*the creditor your collections agent is working for*] to see what type of payment plan or other options the creditor is willing to extend to someone in my position. I want you to know I am doing my best but I have limited resources. I am anxious to get back on track here with my finances and get this debt taken care of . Please explain that to my creditor.

I will call you a week from Tuesday the 19th, then, at 10 am. Is that convenient for you? Thanks... "

Call all bill collectors and creditors in this way, stressing you must be able to *work something out with **all** of them*, something that you can reasonably afford, or you will not be able to pay *anyone*. This will encourage each of them to give you the best pennies-on-the-dollar deal they can squeak out.

Again, **NEVER AGREE TO ANY PAYMENT PLAN, AMOUNT, OR SCHEDULE ON YOUR FIRST CALL!!!** You cannot negotiate with a creditor or collections agent for anything if you agree to pay what they ask of you on your first call.

Sure, they'll offer you maybe no interest for a year, maybe even coupled with an easier payment schedule, but that is not what you want. Or they may offer a small percentage reduction on the total debt if you can pay it in one lump sum. Even if you are prepared to pay down the debt in one lump sum, you know that *50% is the accepted and standard industry starting point*, and any higher amount is unacceptable. What you want is a satisfactory reduction in the debt itself, and if you must make payments, along with lower or no interest, and you need to keep going if you are going to get it. I did it, so I know it can be done. *Just have the patience it takes to complete these steps,* and you will find that you can settle the principal amount of your debt for less, as well as perhaps pay no interest for a year, as well as have an easier payment schedule, if you must make payments. You just need to go through the appropriate process to ask the in the right time in the right way.

     10) The purpose of your second phone call, on the date and time you agreed to call your collections agent or creditor, is to update the collector on your progress. If you are not prepared to continue negotiations yet, for whatever reason, you still must call as agreed to let the collector know you have not yet received a response from some of your other creditors, and then make another phone appointment with him. It is good to stress again that you must be able to make progress with ALL your creditors in order for this to work for you, or bankruptcy is in the future.
     If you are ready to continue, ask the agent what terms the creditor has agreed to extend you. Insert the information into your conversation that your other creditors are very concerned about this, as well. Advise him of any settlement offers you have been made, or of any you "think" they will make you. Do not mention the name of the creditors or the terms, just that offers have been made. If he asks, pause, then tell him you do not

feel at liberty to say.

The objective you want to accomplish with this call is to **make the collector understand he is now in a bidding war with a debtor who has been offered other settlements.** You've already told him your funds are limited, so now he realizes that if he can *quickly* agree to an offer *you* can live with, *he will get his money first.* If he can't make you an offer you can live with, someone else will get the money first. The collector knows that whoever is last in making a satisfactory agreement with you, is left with nothing. You know that he knows this... use it to your advantage and hold out.

At this point you can expect the collector to push for a quick settlement. You may be offered a discount of about 15% to 30%. You already know 50% is the real starting point when going for a lump sum settlement. If you are going for payments, there's no harm in going for a 50% reduction even with the payments. C'mon, you are already not paying the bill, right? So hold out! **When he makes this offer to you, explain to the collector you are finding that most of your other creditors are settling for 50 cents on the dollar, and ask him to go back and talk with your creditor again to see what can be done.** Agree to call him back again on a certain date and time to see what he can offer.

Just hold out, follow the steps according to plan, don't say more than you are supposed to, and you might be surprised. Do NOT offer any more information about the details of the settlements offered to you on that second call either.

Here is a sample of what this second call might sound like....

"Hello, Mr. Jones, this is _____. We spoke a few weeks ago and I told you I would call you today. I am sorry that I do not have good news to report to you. Most of my creditors apparently have no faith in me because they are willing to settle with me for 50 cents on the dollar. Although this is a very generous offer, I simply do not have the cash or the means to pay everyone even at this reduced amount. Please go back to [*your creditor's name*] and see what the absolute best deal they can offer me is. After all this is over I would like to once again be a customer to [*creditor*] obviously on a cash basis. I'll call you in a week from Wednesday so hopefully we can complete this."

AT THIS TIME THE COLLECTOR WILL AGAIN MAKE YOU AN OFFER. DO NOT ACCEPT IT, *IF IT IS NOT WHAT YOU WANT*. (If it is exactly what you wanted, by all means accept it. But it probably won't be what you wanted.) **DO NOT COUNTER-OFFER WITH WHAT YOU REALLY WANT <u>IN THIS PHONE CONVERSATION</u>. DO NOT!!!**

11) This is where you communicate what you consider an acceptable offer to the collector. You must do this before your next scheduled call. This step will show that you are actively and aggressively doing your best to resolve this situation. And, this is where you let them know what will work for you, and what won't.

For maximum effect, this step needs to be done in writing. You will need to either mail or fax it to your collections agent directly, so be sure you've gotten that information – either the direct address or the direct fax number - ahead of time.

You will give the collections agent two options. One of them will be the one you really want, and it will work for both you and the agent. The other will be ridiculous. And you must do it that way for a good reason.

Review the letter samples of **Items C and D** in the section "Letters And Other Samples". Type one out personalized to fit your specific situation and needs. Send or fax it to your collector so he will receive it and have a chance to review it in plenty of time before your next scheduled call. **Make sure the collector has had time to receive and review your letter before you call.**

Call the collection agent at the appointed time. Ask if he had time to review your letter with the creditor. Tell him you are sorry you cannot do better but your current financial condition does not permit it. Remind him again of your situation and stress that your funds are limited. TRY TO SOUND ALMOST A LITTLE UNINTERESTED. If the collector advises you that neither of your offers is acceptable, sound uninterested. "Yeah, ok. Whatever. I am sorry I just don't have the money. If I did, I would pay." Thank him for his time and *begin to say goodbye to hang up.*

DO NOT SUBMIT A SECOND OFFER, as that will imply your first offer was not your true best offer. Simply say no until you get a reduction you can live with. Again... "I am sorry, I just don't have the money. If I did, I would pay." Always justify where you are getting any additional funds from... "I guess I can get my last $90 from my IRA account and close it out." "I suppose I can ask my brother to lend me the $127 I need to satisfy this debt." These sources should be "maybes", not definitive. "I guess I can ask...", or "I suppose I can ...", or "Maybe my uncle will give me ..." *Never admit* you have any assets, anywhere. What you have is your business, no one else's.

12) The MOMENT you and the collection agency agree on the amount and terms of the reduction you *MUST get it verified in writing.* Simply say, "when can I expect to receive a letter to this effect?" If you are told to send in money before that, simply say, "my accountant/wife/husband/attorney will need to see the

amount in writing before he/she releases any funds to me." Or, simply say "No, I need to see this agreement in writing on your official collection agency letterhead, and it must be signed by a person in authority to accept this agreement, before I send anything anywhere". That's the one I used... after all, it IS your money you will be sending.

If your settlement is large, you may also want to request written verification from the creditor. You'll want to know the creditor did agree to this amount as a final and full balance paid, or to the terms you have asked, before you send money. Always put in the memo what the payment is for, and that it is the balance owed paid in full. Don't worry if the collections agent tells you it will take time, tell him that you'll wait. Remember, he knows if he is last, there will be no money left for him. He'll hurry.

Dangling A Carrot
And How To Protect Yourself While Doing It

If you are dealing directly with a creditor, you can increase your chances of making a settlement by "dangling a carrot" in front of them. For this technique to work, you must do a little paperwork and prepare it ahead of time. You send them a letter with a check ahead of time, submitting it to the creditor, or the collections agency. If they deposit the check, it is their approval of the settlement. Sometimes creditors will agree to a reduction which they normally wouldn't, if they are holding a check in their hands.

It is your responsibility to prepare the appropriate paperwork. You will also want to use what is called a "restricted endorsement", although the validity of your claim in court, should the creditor say he did not accept your payment as payment in full, has been in question in some courts. For this reason, also send along a letter of agreement for the creditor to sign.

Note in the sample letter in **Item E - Settlement Letter #3**, that the check number and amount are included in the body of the letter. Also, mail this letter and payment with a service which requires the receiver to sign for the letter, and use a tracking procedure if possible. (Postal certified, return receipt will do fine.) ALWAYS keep copies of your paperwork, including the mailing receipts, AND a copy of *both sides* of the check, after you add the restrictive endorsement below, before you mail it.

Put in the memo of the check, "payment in full for account #4567", or "payment in full for balance with ABC company", or "non-rescindable settlement with ABC company"

Also add, "see reverse". Then on the reverse, write: "RESTRICTIVE ENDORSEMENT: Deposit of this check constitutes an irrevocable agreement for payment in full for all outstanding balances due."

If your settlement on your debt is larger than $2500, it is in your best interest not to use the above method of restricted endorsements *as the only paperwork* to verify the settlement. With amounts greater than this, in some parts of the country it is legal to accept and deposit the payment, and then still pursue the balance owed. An unethical creditor or collections agency, if aware of this, [and very few are] will no doubt pursue the collection if the dollar amount of the balance due warranted it.

What To Do If They Don't Settle
Who To Call And Who To Tell

There are certain instances when you will need to simply bypass certain people. If you find you are dealing with an inexperienced in-house credit manager who is unpredictable, letting emotions instead of logic dictate the decisions made, that is a clear indication you need to create some changes.

You have two choices at this point, and you may need or want to revise your game plan to reflect this. You can either go directly to the in-house collection agent's supervisor (simply make a request to speak to the supervisor while on the phone with the agent) or company president.

Or, you can wait until your debt goes to the next collection level, which would be to a collection agency or attorney. These will always play the negotiation game, and very seldom is it they will not offer you at least 50 cents on the dollar. You see, if they sue you, it could take between 6 and 24 months (depending on the part of the country you are in). If they do win, and you have no money, they must settle for monthly payments anyway. It's a no brainer for them... settle, and move on.

[Editor's Note: the following information was valid at time of original printing of this book in 1999. While some simple details may have changed, usually procedures will not have. However, if you are at this point in negotiations, you may want to seek the professional advice of a qualified credit counselor from a bank, an attorney, or other service.]

If your negotiations become stalemated, it is usually because the creditor will not go any lower. Remember the collections agents and the creditors are playing a psychological game with you, and you must give them a new development to help them save face. Some new topics that will help jumpstart the reduction process again are: 1) you can have a bankruptcy lawyer do the final negotiation, 2) divorce, 3) start the bankruptcy process (a creditor cannot sue you once a bankruptcy has begun, and a bankruptcy can be stopped if timed correctly and once settlements are made), 4) introduce a lawsuit or claim from a much larger creditor into the picture, 5) the IRS always takes preference to other creditors, so auditors will negotiate quickly if they know the IRS is also a creditor.

If A Judgment Is Obtained Against You
Measures You Can Take

It's always better to face your problems head on, and take action by going forward. But if you ignored the letters from the lawyers and collections agencies, you still have some recourse. It can be sometimes more favorable to negotiate a settlement after you are sued. However, if a lawyer obtains a judgment, the collection attorney will have certain rights to collect what the collection agency and the creditor and even the lawyer did not, before the judgment was obtained. The judgment can make the negotiation process difficult but not impossible.

In judgment, a creditor can obtain information from you in a few different ways: 1) By deposition, which is usually held in an attorney's office. You must answer all questions truthfully, and a court reporter will record your responses. 2) By interrogatories, which are written questions the attorney submits to you for a written response. 3) By court examination, which requires your testimony in court. The court decides how much you should pay. 4) By request for a production of documents, in which the debtor is asked to produce specific documents at the attorney's request. This may or may not include a subpoena.

The information the attorney will be looking for will usually be: employment (both full and part time), other sources of income, businesses or business interests you have owned in the last five years, banking information, your spouse's banking information, insurances, vehicles, boats, real estate owned, stocks or securities, mortgages or promissory notes which you either owe or own, judgments you own, jewelry, antiques or collectibles (such as stamp or coin collections), a beneficiary to any trust or will, property transfers in the last five years, other liabilities or assets you now have or will have in the future.

If an attorney cannot seize your tangible assets to collect the debt, he will try to attach your wages. This means a portion of your wages will be paid directly from your employer to your creditor. If you receive two separate attachments, your employer can legally fire you for that reason. [Editor's Note: Again, this law may have changed. Seek advice regarding this from a bankruptcy attorney or someone who would know Human Resource regulations.] You have the right to contest the attachment, but you must be able to prove financial hardship in order to win.

As you can see, if you have let the collection process go this long, you have ignored the collections letters and phone calls to your discredit. Ignoring them won't make them go away, and makes it harder for you to deal with in the long run. If it has gone this far, your alternative is to file for bankruptcy to delay the process. The mistaken belief that an old judgment will not come back to haunt you is unfounded... don't let it happen by judgment proofing yourself and dealing with the problems before they get that far.

Miscellaneous Tips
Secrets To "Tweak" The System In Your Favor

Timing

Timing is very important in your game plan. Creditors and collection agencies are slightly more negotiable towards the end of the month or the end of a quarter. Pace your scheduled calls and contacts to occur at these times, if possible. Avoid January, February and March if possible, as that is when collection activity is heaviest. Businesses have closed the books on their fiscal year, and submitted all their uncollectables to a collection agency. Watch for signs which would make timing appropriate to make your first contact with your creditors, such as new management at the creditor, or an introduction of a new product by the creditor or a competitor that would make the debtor's purchase obsolete. One example would be in September after the coming new year's car models have been introduced.

Ask For A Favorable Credit Rating

When negotiating, it is not out of the question to ask for a favorable credit rating. This is a tool you can use if it seems your offer of 25% or less on the dollar will absolutely not be accepted by the collector. Use this as a bargaining chip if you reach a stalemate in your negotiations. Perhaps this can be part of a letter you write, "getting an increase in my credit card limit to pay you will be necessary for me but I cannot do it with the negative rating you are showing."

Secrecy

Pay all your settlements with a cashiers check or money order drawn from a bank other than where your money is held, or a money order from the post office or convenience store. Getting a money order will indirectly imply you do not even have a bank account.

Your Rights

If a collections agent or creditor has violated your rights, you may have an ace up your sleeve. Here's where you can calmly mention the fact you are aware that the activity they just engaged in is against the law. The creditor or collector may be "embarrassed" to the point of very quickly making a favorable reduction. If they have stepped over the line, ask for a very low pennies-on-the-dollar reduction, after you have made them aware you know what they did was illegal and you know who to report it to... and you don't necessarily have to do that all in one conversation or at one time. Or, you may decide to write a formal letter to the collections agency and creditor to let them know you are considering filing a formal complaint. See **Item F-Harassment Formal Complaint Letter.**

Whenever you are filing a formal complaint to either the creditor or collection agency, always include a copy of the section of the law where they violated your rights. This adds a powerful impact to your letter.

Loose Lips Sink Ships

If you dont' tell them, they usually can't find out and won't know. Be careful what you say! Usually the only thing your creditor knows about you is what is on your original credit application or what you tell them. They cannot legally require you to divulge information about your assets until they have a judgment against you. The creditor may have the right to run a new credit report on you, and in the event of a debt of $10,000 or more, they may check county public records for lawsuits, judgments, or properties you owe.

Toot Your Horn

You can add up the total dollars you've spent with the creditor over the past years. If you have spent $3000 with the creditor over the past years, and are now negotiating for a $300 balance on a $600 debt, how much has the creditor really lost? Fifty cents on the dollar, or 90 cents on the dollar over the life of the account. "Is it worth losing a loyal customer who will obviously go back on a cash basis over 10 cents on the dollar?"

Don't Cry Wolf!

Do not agree to make a lump sum settlement unless you already really have the money!

Attorneys

Collections agencies can be intimidating, but dealing with an attorney can be downright frightening. Remember... the laws are there no matter who writes the letter, and the same laws apply to both collections agencies and attorneys when collecting a debt.

If the collection agency or collection attorney is in another state, they must refer your account to a local attorney for litigation. **Until you decide to definitely proceed with bankruptcy, you are under no obligation to give out any information about who your attorney or accountant is.** If you are asked for your attorney's or accountant's name, don't give it out. If you are asked why you won't, simply say you pay these people by the hour, and since your funds are strictly limited, you cannot afford for them (the collections agent) to run up your bill.

Verify Your Debts

If the debt is very old, or if there has been a change in management, or if the creditor has kept sloppy records, there is a good chance your debt cannot be verified. You should ask for EVERY debt to be verified, as the beginning process of your negotiations. The Debt Collections Practices Act gives consumers the right to have all debts verified. The Act also requires that a collection agency must accomplish this within 30 days, or they cannot continue their collections efforts until the debt is verified. If the debt is too old, or if the creditor does not have enough records to substantiate his claim, or if new management has lost the records, and your debt cannot be verified within 30 days, chances are you will never hear from the collections agency again.

IMPORTANT NOTE HERE: it is HERE, and **HERE ONLY** that you can take immediate advantage of this fact and erase this debt from your credit record and credit history file. **YES, it really can be done, even if the debt *was* real.** However, *DON'T be fooled* by the scams of people who tell you they can erase "all" negative credit from your report. You see, because of this law, they can, but it will be wiped off for only 30 days, and THEN GO RIGHT BACK ON when it has been "verified". If you request a second verification of the debt, and then dispute it, if within another 30 days it cannot be substantiated, the law requires it to be removed from your credit history file. The timing is critical in this sequence, and the steps must be followed exactly. The wording of your requests is also important.

Debt verification is a good technique to delay the collections process or to delay a first contact with a creditor or collections agency in your game plan, if you are waiting for the proper timing or avoiding January, February, and March. See **Item G - Letter Of Dispute Of A Debt**.

Use the up-to-date information in Chapter 6 of this book to look for the correspondence addresses, the phone number to call, or the online address to request your reports.

Two Debts Are Better Than One

Sometimes two different creditors will submit a claim for a debt you owe to the same collections agency. If the same collection agent does not get both accounts, you will definitely want to make the two agents aware of this. Collections agencies all strive to reduce the cost of collections, and will want to merge both collections to just one agent. This is good for you, because it strengthens your argument that you have no money, when the agency sees that you have two separate debts which they are collecting for. It also makes it easier for you to negotiate, since you are then not pitting one collector against another in the same agency.

Statue Of Limitations

Every state has one, and only a bankruptcy lawyer can tell you what it is for your state. In many states, debts which are older than four years can't be brought up for suit.

Verbatim Is Bad

Whatever you do, make an effort to change the words in the letter samples and phone scripts, before you use them, while still keeping the idea intact and integrity of the material coherent. If everyone who reads this book, and who reads the material from the Debt Reduction And Credit Consultant Institute uses the same letters and same words, the collections agencies may have run across these same words and letters before, and will soon realize they are dealing with someone who knows all the tricks. This is NOT good for you, as they will be less likely to deal you a reduction in your debts then, knowing you are playing their game and may resort to bankruptcy eventually anyway. Always change the words of the letters, but keep the meaning.

HOW TO HANDLE ABUSES AND WHO TO REPORT THEM TO

Who To Tell

The Fair Debt Collection Practices Act sets specific guidelines about what collections agencies, creditors, and lawyers who are trying to collect a debt from you are allowed to do and what they are not. Those who have been found to violate the Act can be fined large amounts, up to $10,000 a day, for each violation. You can read a copy of the Act at the link in the last section of this book, "Copies Of Existing Laws". Take some time to go through this information, as you will see there are many things which were written in your favor. Know the law and you will be more prepared to deal with the collections agents and creditors.

The Federal Trade Commission is responsible for overseeing the enforcement of the Fair Debt Collection Practices Act, and the FTC is the organization to report abuses to. State law conforms to federal law, and when reporting a violation you will want to file the complaint with the attorney general of your state or a similar state protection agency. Complaints must be filed to the FTC within 30 days of the violation, and if you choose, under the Fair Debt Collection Practices Act, to file a civil lawsuit, it must be filed within one year of the violation. A listing of FTC offices and addresses can be found at the end of this chapter.

List Of Abuses Which Are Not Allowed According To The Law

Listed here are some of the unfair debt collection practices which anyone who is attempting to collect a debt is prohibited from engaging in:

the collector cannot

>>>write to anyone other than the debtor or the debtor's attorney or representative. They may, however, try to find the debtor. They are allowed to ask others where the debtor is, but cannot reveal the reason that they are trying to collect an unpaid bill from them.
>>>use abusive or profane language or behavior to "harass, oppress, or abuse any person".
>>>threaten violence or harm to property or reputation
>>>cannot use the telephone to continually annoy, by calling and hanging up, calling and not identifying themselves, or repeated calls.
[*Note: I experienced this myself. The caller never revealed he was calling due to the debt, but called about 5 times a day and pretended to be looking for someone else... the same person all the time. I wondered why the same idiot would call the same number and ask for the same person who would never be there! I never realized it was the collector, till one day, after I began my training in this information, I told the caller I knew who he was, asked the caller not to call again and mentioned to the caller I was considering filing a report to the FTC for his*

violations of the Fair Debt Collection Practices Act, and I never got another call again. Though I had a good idea, I really didn't know *exactly* who the caller was, but... did it matter?]

>>> call the debtor during inconvenient hours. The only hours allowed for calls is between 8 am and 9 pm, unless the debtor specifically agrees to another time without those parameters. No more than two calls a week are allowed.

>>> advertise, publish, or distribute a "deadbeat" list of debtors who owe money, and this includes telling people, aside from putting it in print. (This is why you will sometimes see local businesses with a sign out in front of their property or posted in their store which reads, "Looking for *a person's name*" The retailer cannot post a sign saying the person wrote a bad check, claimed a charge was fraud when it wasn't, or used a fraudulent credit card, but that is what that sign means. The retailer is not "telling people" about the debtor, but is warning other retailers who would know or be able to figure out what the sign means.)

>>>contact the debtor by using a postcard or other means such as a letterhead which indicates the recipient owes a debt, or that the sender is a collection agency attempting to collect a debt.

>>> make the debtor pay for any collect calls made to them, or for any other expenses in communicating with them. (no collect calls, and if a collection agency ever leaves a message on your answering machine which asks you to return the call, and it is not an 800 or other toll free number, that is a violation!)

>>>contact the debtor at the debtors place of employment if the employer does not permit it.

>>> use any means such as a fictitious name or any other deceit to imply the collector is a law firm, or misrepresent themselves to be a credit bureau,

government agency, either verbally or in writing.
>>>threat to arrest.
>>>ask for a postdated check. A debtor may offer one, but the collections agency may not ask for one. If one is issued, the collections agency must give three days written notification upon cashing the check.
>>>use funds sent to the agency in a way not agreed upon by the collector and the debtor.
>>>threaten legal action unless they plan to actually take legal action.
>>>continue to contact the debtor after the debtor has specifically notified them to stop.

(Use this one carefully... the collection agency may notify you just once more, and then since you prohibit them from contacting you again, their only alternative would be to take legal action, or they may choose to forget the whole thing. You may be specific in your request, such as, "do not call me on the telephone anymore". This leaves them open to still contact you by mail, and therefore you delay legal action by them, if that is something you do not want to initiate.)

Warning: the Fair Debt Collections Practices Act *does not apply to the IRS, at least not in real life.* **Do not** attempt to use any of the information contained in this book to reduce back taxes owed. Taxes and the IRS are an entirely separate monster. Although the information about dealing with the IRS was taught to me, I will refrain from relaying it here due to the fact many of the laws dealing with the IRS change every year. If you need to deal with back taxes owed to the IRS, I will tell you they can be negotiated. However, seek the advice of a competent attorney, one who specifically handles those types of cases.

How To Handle The Violations

Begin by reading the laws of the Fair Debt & Credit Reporting Act (FDCRA). You will find a web address with access to it at the end of this section. Go to the law, print it out, and keep a copy. Familiarize yourself with the law.

There are four types of individuals you will be dealing with when having contact with collections agencies: 1) a creditor's employee who works in the collections department, 2) an attorney, 3) experienced employees of third party collections agencies, and 4) inexperienced employees of third party collections agencies.

Of this group, the lawyers will give you the least trouble. Typically they conduct themselves in a business-like manner at all times, as they do not wish to jeopardize their license to practice law. If a lawyer ever does engage in an unfair debt collection practice against you, besides reporting him to the FTC and your state attorney general, you may also report him to your state's law bar.

The in-house collection agent is an individual working in the collections department of the creditor, and will typically call you with a pre-written script. If you have any difficulty with this person, just ask to speak to the credit dept. supervisor. If you still can't get anywhere, write or call the company president.

If you have difficulty with collections agency employees, complaints should be sent to the FTC, your state attorney general or the state protection agency set up for that purpose, and the collection agency owner, as well as the creditor who hired the company. You will find the experienced agents - those with seven or more years of experience - usually are well aware of how far they can go and do not violate the law. The inexperienced employees are typically the offenders, and are the most volatile. If a collector gets out of hand, immediately file all the prescribed reports, and also contact your local police department, if it is warranted.

Federal Trade Commissions Access Information

FTC Headquarters
Corresponding Branch:

Federal Trade Commission
Consumer Response Center
600 Pennsylvania Avenue, NW
Washington, DC 20580

202-326-2222
Toll Free: 877-382-4357

Online access:

www.ftc.gov

That address will take you to the home site, from which you can explore for your desired information.

If you have a complaint, you can access the Complaint Form which can be filled out online from the button at the home page, or type into your browser the direct address:

https://rn.ftc.gov/pls/dod/wslocq$.startup?Z_ORG_CODE=PU01

To find different offices or other information regarding contacting the FTC, use:

http://www.ftc.gov/ftc/contact/shtm

(You can also access the National Do Not Call Registry from this page, as well as get information regarding Identity Theft, online spam and phishing.)

Chapter 5

LETTERS AND OTHER SAMPLES

On the following pages you will find all of the worksheets, samples of letters, and other miscellaneous items you will need to gather up and have prepared and ready to access in negotiating your debt. You will need to re-type some of these into your computer and print several copies for your use. Be sure when sending letters that you personalize them, and print only one copy at a time personalized for the person you are sending it to with correct date and names in place.

ITEM A - NET WORTH WORKSHEET
~~~~~~

Assets...........Amount $_____

Cash On Hand............$_____

Bank Accounts

Savings.......…………..$_____

Account Number_____

Account Number_____

Checking......………….$_____

Account Number_____

Account Number_____

Account Number_____

SUBTOTAL (A) …..$_____

Insurance Policies

Policy Number_____

Insurance Company _____

Cash Value........$_____

      Policy Number_____

Insurance Company _____

Cash Value………$_____

SUBTOTAL (B) ………..$_____

Securities And Bonds

    Account Number_____

    Broker_____

Value……………………….$_____

    Account Number_____

Broker_____

Value……………………….$_____

Account Number_____

Broker_____

Value………,,,,,,,,,,,,,,,,,,,,……….$_____

SUBTOTAL (C) ………..$_____

Real Estate

    Description_____

    Estimated Value………………… $_____

    Description_____

Estimated Value.............. $_____

    Description_____

Estimated Value………...$_____

SUBTOTAL (D) ....$_____

Jewelry

    Description_____

Estimated Value............... $_____

    Description_____

Estimated Value……………. $_____

    Description_____

Estimated Value…………. $_____

SUBTOTAL (E) ....$_____

Automobiles

    Year_____
    Make _____
    Model_____
    Estimated Value………… $_____

    Year_____
    Make _____
    Model_____

Estimated Value.......... $_____

Year_____
Make _____
Model_____
Estimated Value............ $_____

SUBTOTAL (F) ....$_____

Other Assets
Description_____
Value............$_____

Description_____
Value............$_____

Description_____
Value...........$_____

Description_____
Value..........$_____

Description_____
Value.........$_____

SUBTOTAL (G) ....$_____

ADD TOTAL ASSETS (A+B+C+D+E+F+G)

TOTAL ASSETS (H) ....$_____

~~~~~~
Liabilities (DEBTS)
~~~~~~

Creditor...........................Balance (Amount Owed)

_____
$_____

_____
$_____

_____
$_____

_____
$_____

_____
$_____

_____
$_____

_____
$_____

_____
$_____

_____
$_____

_____
$_____

$_____

$_____

ADD TOTAL LIABILITIES (I)...$_____

FIND YOUR NET WORTH....

TOTAL ASSETS (H)...............$_____

(minus) -

TOTAL LIABILITIES (I) ....$_____

(equal) =

NET WORTH.....$_____

+++

ITEM B - PERSONAL BUDGET WORKSHEET

Complete this form EVERY MONTH to determine where your money is going and to see if you can reduce/redistribute expenses.

INICOME
Salaries ....$_____
Wages................$_____
Dividends............$_____
Interest................$_____
Rentals ....$_____
Alimony...............$_____
Other...................$_____

TOTAL INCOME $_____

FIXED EXPENSES
Food......................$_____
Housing.................$_____
Utilities..................$_____
Transportation........$_____
Maintenance..........$_____
Furnishings............$_____
Clothing.................$_____
Installment
Purchases.............$_____
Personal Care.........$_____
Insurance Premiums.$_____
Medical &
Dental Care.............$_____

Education................$_____
Taxes (all kinds).......$_____
Other....................... $_____

TOTAL FIXED EXPENSES.......$_____

TOTAL AVAILABLE

Income..………………..$_____

(minus) –

Fixed Expenses………..$_____

(equal) =

TOTAL AVAILABLE .....$_____

Variable expenses...........
        Entertainment.................$_____
        Recreations....................$_____
        Vacations.......................$_____
        Investments....................$_____
        Savings..........................$_____
        Other.............................$_____

TOTAL VARIABLE EXPENSES…………………..$_____

TOTAL AVAILABLE…...$_____

(minus) –

TOTAL VARIABLE EXPENSES….…..........$_____

(equal) = TOTAL END OF MONTH AVAILABLE

$_____

+++

ITEM C - SETTLEMENT LETTER #1, OUT OF COURT SETTLEMENT

Use This Sample To Send To Collection Agencies

Client's Name
Client's Address
City, State, Zip
Account Number
Date

Mr. (Collector)
Name Of Collection Agency
Address Of Collection Agency
City, State, Zip

Dear Sir;

It has been a pleasure working with you. As you are aware, due to my recurring employment problem, [*or whatever else you told him*] , resulting from my poor health, I find it regrettably out of my reach to pay my debts to your fine company. My present modest income is barely enough for me to survive on, leaving nothing for back payments. Unfortunately, I have nothing of value to sell in order to raise cash and satisfy my obligation with your or a host of other creditors in your same position.

However, I feel obligated to your company and am willing to offer a settlement of 25 cents on the dollar as payment in full. My current balance with you is $1,425. I have two repayment plans I can realistically complete.

    a) I am able to make my $356.25 payment in full (25% of $1,425) next Friday,
    [*or two Fridays from now, whatever is realistic for*

you] after I cash my paycheck, or

     b) 36 monthly payments of $39.58

If these terms are acceptable to you , please sign where indicated and return to me immediately. Please circle which payment plan you prefer.

Yours truly,

(SIGNATURE)
Your name here

Read, Approved, and Accepted by:
_____ Date_____

++

ITEM D - SETTLEMENT LETTER #2, OUT OF COURT SETTLEMENT

Use This Sample To Send To Creditors

Client's Name
Client's Address
City, State, Zip
Account Number
Date

Mr. (Collector)
Name Of Collection Agency
Address Of Collection Agency
City, State, Zip

Dear Sir;

As a result of my recent divorce, [*or whatever you told him*] , regrettably, I find myself in a difficult financial situation for the first time in my life, where I am unable to satisfy my debt with your fine company. Unfortunately, after the divorce I was left with no savings account or items of value which I could sell in order to raise the necessary funds to satisfy your debt, as well as all the other creditors debts.

Even though most of the charges incurred in your store were from my former spouse, I find myself compelled to make a settlement with you. I would be willing to pay you my balance of $850 in the following fashion:

Option 1: Initiate one lump sum payment of $400 for balance in full.

Option 2: Payment Plan:
>January 1, 200_: $35
>February 1, 200_: $35
>[*and so on and so forth till the balance due is paid*]
>August 1, 200_: $35, final payment

Please indicate which of these terms are acceptable, please sign below and forward to me at once. Even though some of my friends who have been in this same position have filed for bankruptcy, I am avoiding this, since I feel it is not the correct thing to do.

Yours truly,

(SIGNATURE)
Your name here

Read, Approved, and Accepted by:
_____ Date_____

++

ITEM E - Settlement Letter #3, Out Of Court Settlement

Use This Sample When Sending Your Payment Ahead Of Acceptance

Client's Name
Client's Address
City, State, Zip
Account Number
Date

Mr. (Collector)
Name Of Creditor Or Collection Agency
Address Of Collection Agency
City, State, Zip

Dear Mr. _____;

Please find enclosed my check # 162 in the amount of $234. This check is tendered on the express condition of acceptance of the settlement in the disputed claim. Endorsement of this check by you or your client, [*name of creditor*] , or both shall affect a full release, accord and satisfaction of this debt. If you or [*creditor*] do not agree to accept these terms, *you are instructed to return the check immediately.*

If you have any questions, please do not hesitate to call.

Yours truly,

(SIGNATURE)
Your name here
+++

Item F - Harassment Formal Complaint Letter

Use This Sample When Writing To A Collector
About Their Unlawful Collections Practices

Your name
Your address
City, State, Zip

Date

Collections Agency Or Creditor
Address
City, State, Zip

Gentlemen;

Please be advised I am in the process of preparing a formal complaint to the Federal Trade Commission, [*list their local address here*] , regarding the illegal collection tactics used by your firm.

These tactics include, but are not limited to: [*specifically cite the incident here, or simply list : intimidation, threats, verbal abuse, lying and even blackmail.*] All incidents have been carefully documented and I am prepared to testify in any civil action my lawyer chooses to initiate.

Regarding my open balance with you, the correct amount is $_____ and not the fabricated sum of $_____ you are requesting. [*only include this sentence if it applies, of course.*]

I am notifying you not to make any more phone calls to

me. Please govern yourselves accordingly.

Cordially,

(SIGNATURE)
Your name here

+++

ITEM G - LETTER OF DISPUTE OF A DEBT

Use This Sample To Send To A Collections Agency Or Creditor, Or Lawyer

Your name
Your address
City, State, Zip

Date

Collections Agency Or Creditor Or Lawyer
Address
City, State, Zip

RE: (your name) Vs. (your creditors name), your file no. 1234-56

I am in receipt of your letter of June 9, 200_, regarding the subject matter.

My records show that this account is not as you indicate, and that it [*put here " has been paid in full", or "shows a different balance", or simply say "is already settled" Or, be specific, if you have specific data about the incorrect content of the letter.*]. I am therefore disputing this alleged debt and ask that you provide me with written verification and clarification of this claim.

Very truly yours,

(SIGNATURE)
Your name here
++

Chapter 6

RESOURCES

The Law Pertaining To Debt Collection

These laws will not be printed here, as space does not allow. (The actual manuscript would take about 800 pages in this book!) I STRONGLY recommend you connect to the link of this law on the Internet and print out or copy and paste into your computer files. This first link is actually a commentary regarding the law, and relates much of the important information as well as any updates.

Take some time to read this commentary! It is tedious, but you will find some very VERY interesting data in it regarding you, your credit, and your debt.

Below is the link address so you may input it into your Internet browser to access the law and print it out.

The Fair Debt Collection Practices Act

http://www.ftc.gov/os/statutes/fdcpa/commentary.htm

A Truly FREE Credit Report

If you have fallen for the TV commercial singing about a freecreditreport.com, or the one showing the young guy who is down on his luck because he didn't know what was in his credit report, you just might fall for the temptation to either call or go online to register and get a credit report sent to you.

What you don't know (but you should be able to guess by now) is the credit report is definitely NOT free, and if you consent to receiving it, you will be locked in to getting binged (charged) on your debit or credit card for the rest of your life (if they can get away with it) for that service.

To remove the service, it just about takes an act of God. You have to have ALL the information that you provided them with, AND the information they provided you with, as well as know your SS# (easy for you, but may not be easy if you have a spouse try to do this for you, if you fall ill or whatever), AND… it *absolutely cannot be done if the person who engaged in the service is not the one speaking on the line when the service is cancelled.* What this means is that if you called to have a report for you and your spouse sent, then you want to cancel, you will EACH have to make a separate phone call to remove the service.

If you had this recurring service (which is what it is) put on a credit card that you later want to cancel, and you cancel your card, the recurring service will still occur and the card will remain open unless you go through the steps required to cancel the service first.

The government allows for one (truly!) free credit report per person, per year, and it can be obtained by

requesting it online at:
www.annualcreditreport.com

Or you may call the official access phone number at 1/877-322-8228 . After going through a simple verification process over the phone, your reports will be mailed to you within 15 days, allowing 2 – 3 weeks for delivery.

You may also write to request your credit report by mail at:
Annual Credit Report Request Service
PO Box 105281
Atlanta, GA 30348-5281

The same applies, your reports will be mailed to you within 15 days, and you should allow 2 – 3 weeks for delivery.

You will receive one report from each of the three credit services, authorized by the government to relay this information to you. The current address (as of this printing) for each of the three credit reporting agencies are included below. Use these addresses when writing letters to verify a debt, after receiving your free credit reports. (These addresses are changed often by the agencies, so always be sure, if you do this each year, you validate the address first before mailing your information. That is easy to do by calling the toll-free number. Also, any bank should be able to give them to you.)

Experian
PO Box 2002
Allen, TX 75013
Toll Free: 888-397-3742

TransUnion
PO Box 1000
Chester, PA 19022
Toll Free: 800-888-4213

Equifax
PO Box 740241
Atlanta, GA 30374
Toll Free: 800-685-1111

Section III

Keeping Your Personal Energy Free

In Conclusion

There has never been a better time than NOW to begin getting your life turned around. If you are up to your eyeballs in debt, it will BE a turnaround in that it will take constant, vigilant action from you, and one which requires commitment from you. Not because it is hard to do, but because it is necessary to be focused and consistent. You must be consistent in your debt elimination activities and make sure you write the appropriate letters and make the necessary calls at exactly the correct times.

When examining your options for realigning your thoughts and understanding of spending and money, I strongly suggest you consider the book **Your Money Or Your Life**. You will then have two tools to use to 1) get you out of the debt you are in and 2) see to it you do not get back into it.

Anyone who is in debt is putting themselves in a position to be under the thumb of the person or company they are in debt to. Aside from promising away your future energy to pay for what you have now, you are a modern slave to the creditor you owe. You are at their mercy. In this day and age it may not seem important, but in the future, if this country's financial system is in turmoil, being in or out of debt may make a big difference in who is truly free and who is not.

May God, whatever you perceive God to be, be with you and bless your efforts. Ask, and you SHALL receive... no matter who doesn't like it.

Suggested Reading

Any of these books can be purchased right now on line by accessing the link to Amazon
at : http://www.amazon.com

Your Money Or Your Life: Transforming Your Relationship With Money And Achieving Financial Independence; written by Joe Dominguez and Vicki Robin; published by Penguin Books

You'll See It When You Believe It; written by Dr. Wayne Dyer, published by Avon Books

Left-Brain Finance For Right-Brain People: A Money Guide For The Creatively Inclined; written by Paula Ann Monroe; published by Sourcebooks, Inc.

Life Strategies: Doing What Works, Doing What Matters; written by Phillip C. McGraw, Ph.D; published by Hyperion

The Millionaire Next Door; written by Thomas J. Stanley, Ph.D, and William D. Danko, Ph. D; published by Longstreet Press

NOTES

NOTES

NOTES

www.ingramcontent.com/pod-product-compliance
Ingram Content Group UK Ltd.
Pitfield, Milton Keynes, MK11 3LW, UK
UKHW051254180426
11947UKWH00020B/1714